Learning the Rules

by Clare O'Brien

I need to know these words.

classroom

library

lockers

project

rules

Rule 1 • Keep the classroom clean.
Rule 2 • Put away the supplies.
Rule 3 • Listen when someone speaks.
Rule 4 • Read quietly in the library.
Rule 5 • Stay in line.
Rule 6 • Throw away trash.
Rule 7 • Keep things in a locker.
Rule 8 • Study in class.
Rule 9 • Be on time.

supplies

The classroom is a place to learn. Some rules help us learn. Some rules help us work with others.

▲ Many rules help us learn.

We must follow the rules in the classroom. One rule tells us to keep the classroom clean.

▲ This boy follows a rule.

We must listen to our classmates.
This girl reads to the class.
We listen to the girl.

 We must listen in class.

Today someone visits our class.
We listen to the visitor.

Title I
Chamberlain Elementary
428 N. 5th St.
Goshen, IN 46528

✓ Rule #3

Listen when someone speaks.

▲ We are listening.

Our class visits the library. We read books. We must read quietly in the library.

✓ Rule #4
Read quietly in the library.

▲ We must not talk in the library.

We go to lunch. The rule tells us to stay in line.

Rule #5

Stay in line.

▲ We must stay in line.

We clean up when we finish our lunch. This girl throws away her trash.

✓ Rule #6
Throw away trash.

▲ The rule tells us to throw away trash.

We have lockers. We must keep our things in our lockers.

Rule #7

Keep things in a locker.

▲ This girl keeps things in the locker.

We study in class. We read in class. We learn math, too.

✓ **Rule #8**
Study in class.

▲ One rule tells us to study in class.

We must start our work on time.
We must finish our work on time.

Rule #9

Be on time.

▲ One rule tells us to be on time.

We have rules at school.
The rules help us learn.

Rules We Learned

✓ Rule 1 • Keep the classroom clean.
✓ Rule 2 • Put away the supplies.
✓ Rule 3 • Listen when someone speaks.
✓ Rule 4 • Read quietly in the library.
✓ Rule 5 • Stay in line.
✓ Rule 6 • Throw away trash.
✓ Rule 7 • Keep things in a locker.
✓ Rule 8 • Study in class.
✓ Rule 9 • Be on time.